I had a friend who was a fox. She would run infront of my car in the early mornings on my route to work at the farm. I had a feeling she was playing, like dolphins jumping infront of a boat.
She didn't know she was my friend. She didn't get to smell me or look into my eyes. But I felt connected with her.
Last week as I passed her home I saw her laying on the ground. She had tried her game with a car that was driving too fast.
I got out of my car and picked up her warm body, thinking she would spring to life and nip me, as if this were another one of her tricks. The energy of her muscles was still vibrating under her thick fur.
I laid her down in the tall grass by the side of the road. A better place to rest than pavement.
I can't stop thinking about her now. Her power in death is just as strong as it was in life.

Power, after all, is not attached only to matter. Memories can be just as real, just as important, just as comforting, as the soul that left us behind.
Eternity is just another place to leap into with curiosity and wonder.
It will be.
at the moment of my death I hope I am playing too. I hope I die still reaching for the next bank like my friend the fox, and I hope I can be as beautiful when my breath turns to wind.
When I die I want the memory of my bones scattered in wet grass and for my friends to wonder if this is
another one of my tricks.
The burning torch of my story will just change hands.

A person close to me recently suggested that I needed to leave my past behind me, to get over it and stop letting old stuff ruin otherwise good moments. He said those dreaded and loaded words: "stop being a victim." After an evening of having fun and hanging out, I began talking about a memory I felt was relevant to some aspect of our conversation. I don't remember exactly what it was that provoked this response but it had to do with bringing up a particular past long-term relationship where I was emotionally tortured and physically harmed to explain some of my strange behaviors and lingering fears. Usually when I mention this time of my life in conversation I am trying to better connect with a person, to let them know where I'm coming from. I still don't have the words to put that experience into an emotional story with a narrative so I don't. When I talk about that time it is only to share how my life changed as a result.

Nevertheless, showing my scars puts me in a very vulnerable place. I don't let people into the specifics of my past unless I trust them so being shut down in that way was alarming. My friend's words haunted me and sparked many weeks of questioning myself and my attitude towards past trauma. What if I was mistaking processing for wallowing? What if I was mistaking opening up with lingering on shit that nobody has the energy or desire to hear? I think of myself as strong and resilient, able to survive in horrific conditions, but what if talking about those times actually proved I wasn't? I have what if the best way to heal is to try to just forget about it all? Or at least fake it until I get there?

The interesting thing is that my brain has actually blocked out a lot events that happened during that abusive relationship and a lot of what I can remember is blurry and shadowed. Many people are apparently familiar with this subconscious survival tactic. Sometimes when I'm least expecting it, an image of something I had forgotten pops into my mind. A whole event or a tiny weird detail. I don't think I have any control over it. What then would it mean to let go of (or suppress or ignore) those already existing memories and my evolving response to them? What would it involve to keep what is still buried buried?

I started thinking about whether or not I would indeed choose to forget the hard things that have happened to me if I had the option. I would never say that experiencing trauma has made me a better person because I could have been an equally good person without shedding so many tears. It would have been pretty nice to have spent my early twenties partying or writing a novel or something instead of spending it in a black hole. However, I do know that the abuse I went through enables me to deeply empathize with others going through similar types of things. The insight that pain brings has given me the responsibility and fuel to try to better the world in the small ways I can. Although the awful things I have experienced do make me move through the world differently than others, I'm not sure I would want to erase my memory of them. They are a part of me, inseparable from my wholeness.

Besides, making peace with the past is precisely how it hurts less. Taking a combative stance against certain experiences usually only gives them power. I've found that when I hold painful memories with tenderness they become lighter. This is not to say that I don't still feel a great sadness- sometimes that is an appropriate response- but that I accept the past and all the feelings that go along with it. I can hold them and let them exist while at the same time feel joy and contentment with my present life. Perhaps all conscious and aware living things have an ongoing ache on some level. Yet we can still go on.

Talking is a valid and important part of healing for so many people and being heard is essential for our survival. Telling me, or anyone else who has suffered or is still visibly suffering, that we need to contain and monitor that suffering in some way is not helpful. Likewise, charging someone with "being a victim" when they are recounting past events doesn't take into consideration the complexity of the situation. Survivor/victim is a false dichotomy; really, if a person is still alive after being victimized by an abuser, they are automatically a survivor. You can qualify as a survivor at every stage of you healing process, even if you are sometimes a mess. Even if you sometimes let you friends know what you've been through and are still affected by. Maybe especially then.

Depression is hard to argue with.
By definition, it is all encompassing,
almost impossible to see out of.
Maybe write your future self a note.
Having a letter in your own writing to remind yourself
that other moods or ways of being exist
could come in useful during that future time
when everything turns pale.

dear future self...

Write this note whenever you feel
a spark of joy, or just contentment,
or just during a time
when you don't want to die as much.
Give yourself the tangible proof
that life never stays stagnant for too long,
that minds, like the ocean, ebb and flow.

I have this goat head that a coworker gave me sitting in a garbage bag on my lawn.
When I got it, She had been recently killed. The hair was clean and her eyes were only just turning milky.
Now the bag is deflated and heavy.
I initially kept it outside because there was snow on the ground but after a few weeks of warmer weather I am afraid to open it.
The smell is one reason, the mess another.
(me, ignoring the goat.)

I have this goat head that a coworker gave me sitting in a garbage bag on my lawn.
When I got it, She had been recently killed. The hair was clean and her eyes were only just turning milky.
Now the bag is deflated and heavy.
I initially kept it outside because there was snow on the ground but after a few weeks of warmer weather I am afraid to open it.
The smell is one reason, the mess another.
(me, ignoring the goat.)

Its hard not to see this situation as a metaphor. for my emotional life.
GUILT
sadness
Anxiety
regret
Shame
Put things (dead animals or feelings) in bags and hope they decompose on their own until I can take the bones out clean and white to put on a shelf in my room.
Of course, thats not how it works. I will have to cut the bag open eventually and air it out so the environment can do its thing.
I will have to look at the decay in the face. Time has made it uglier than if I cared for it immediately.
ok
...here it goes

To my great suprise, maggots had gotten through the plastic and tended to the head before I could.
There was no goop or blood. The bugs didn't swarm over me. The skull didn't even smell. Really, in its decay the goat was still beautiful.
I don't know why it took me so long to untie the bag. The natural process that happens after death isn't something to be scared of.
So maybe this ordeal is a different type of metaphor than I had anticipated. Is it now a stretch to think that it is ok to keep things on hold until I am ready to look at them face to face?
Perhaps it is silly to find alternative meanings in everything I do and this experience has only to do with a decaying goat and nothing more. However, I've found that lessons learned after this much psychological build up tend to apply in other areas of life as well. So I'm going to go ahead and not worry as much about the things I suppress. I want to trust that when my brain and heart are ready, they will uncover what needs to be worked out. This process can neither be rushed or avoided forever. Healing happens in its own time.

What would it mean to claim our brokenness,
to be ok with growing
while not ever completely healing,
to even maybe find our wounds beautiful?
What would it mean to flaunt the strength in our pain,
to celebrate the unique skills we have in survival,
to be proud of our messy lives
and the ways we did not die?
Trauma does not end at tragedy.
We who have suffered
are brilliant dreamers of new futures
nobody thought possible.
We have already learned how live through apocalypse.
We will be the leaders at the end of the world.

I WANT TO FEEL AT PEACE WITH/in MY BODY
I want to live a life of pleasure and vibrancy.
I want to love myself unconditional
and learn what it means to
inhabit my breath.
truly

I often feel disconnected from my body. Even though it has carried me up mountains, gives me pleasure in sunshine and in the cool water of creeks, and lets me hold my loved ones close, I so often want to crawl out of my skin and remember what it feels like to breathe without lungs. My body has done so much for me and always does the best it can yet I feel like it weighs me down more than it enables me to participate in the world. This, of course, cant really be true. I am my body; without it I wouldn't exist, or at least not in this realm. Maybe I just want another one. I'd rather be a jaguar or perhaps some sort of whale. Or maybe I really just want to be less markedly female, to have a body that isn't sexualized and commodified every time I leave my bedroom.

My friend and I had a conversation the other day about our experiences of being labeled female at birth. For both of us it has been the source of so much pain. Gender binaries are limiting for all humans but to move through society with a body that is seen as woman [illegible] is dangerous. It has always been. I asked my friend if not relating to and pushing back against femininity and all that it represents affects how she identifies. She replied that while she/her pronouns have begun to make her uncomfortable, she wonders if it is primarily due to internalized misogyny. I related to this a lot. How much of my relationship with my body has to do with how it is perceived in society instead of my own awareness in it? How joyful it would be to live in a community where bodies didn't carry so much imposed gendered meaning?

It seems impossible to know what truly being a woman means outside of patriarchy but I want to imagine towards that future. I've slowly started a practice of marveling instead of judging when I look into a mirror. I try to wonder at my body as if it were a flower or a leaf. I praise the memories caught in the scars on my legs, the passing of time etching my face, and the abundance that delicious meals left on my thighs. I represent one of the billions of beautiful forms that nature creates out of earth. How lucky to participate in this world full of other unique living things!

My body is innocent in my battle of figuring out how to live in it. Regardless of how others may see it and despite how others may react because of that perception, I want learn how to make peace with it. Having a body should be simple and expressing a gender (or none) should be fun. I am getting bored of spending my so much of my life feeling trapped. My body, like all bodies, really does deserve to be loved.

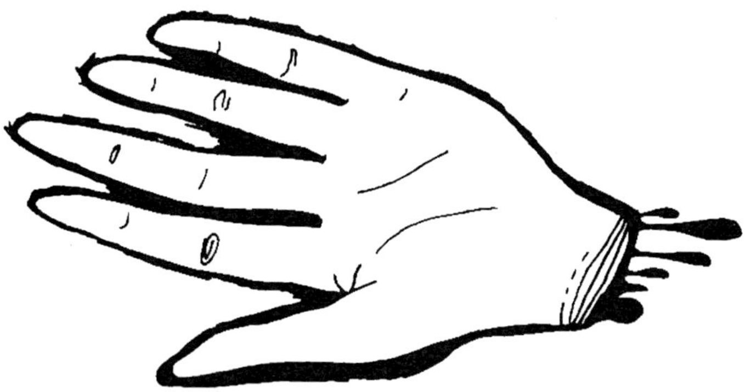

The body is the first holder of opression,
but also the source of original power.
Everything comes back to its waters.
Your bones cast a wide net
carrying everything you've done
or had done to you.
Love it because
it's doing the best it can.

hugs are good
for your health
too good not to Share

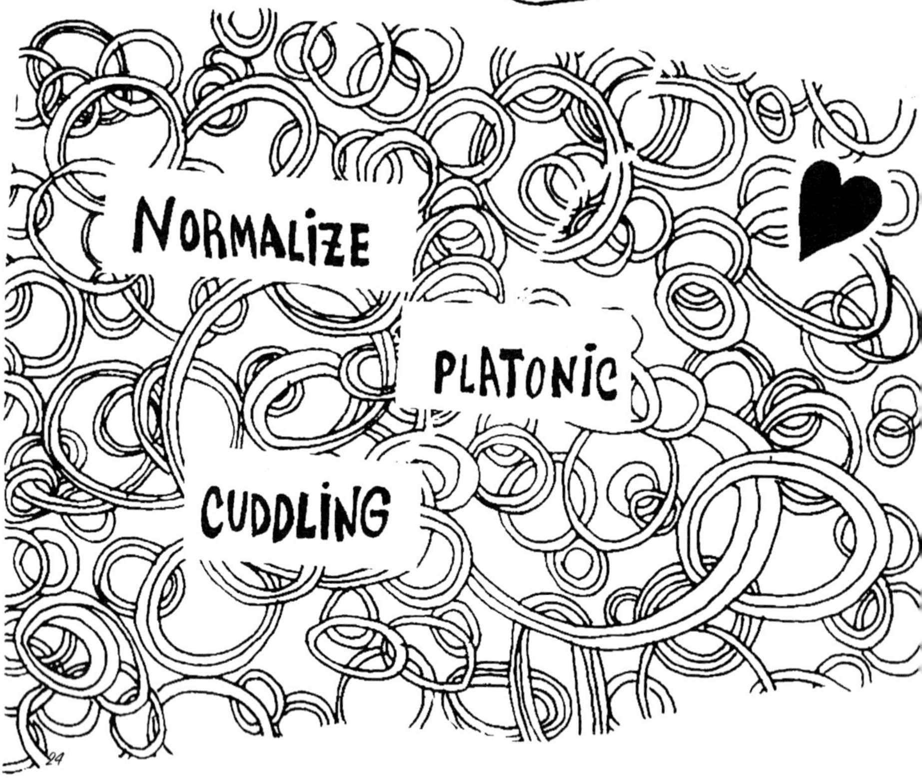
NORMALIZE
PLATONIC
CUDDLING

When I get up in the morning. I feel like I'm being Chased.
I rush to get dressed and go to work.
ONCE I'm there I'm OK.
But the feeling Starts to return on the drive home.
The chase happens across space-time. I know moving quickly won't gain distance but still I try.
Sometimes, when I take a nap, It
The claws of sorrow and despair. I can't move when I awake.

Really, it's phone calls with friends that let me outrun the feeling for enough time to relax.
I've also found that I can hide in sunshine for a while.
Whiskey and a good book help also but they mostly just distract from noticing how close it is getting.
What if it finally catches me?
It's happened before. It's almost relieving, to no longer have to run, to sink into the hot embrace of depression.
It is familiar. It is easy to let go.
But then it isn't. Everything becomes more difficult; talking, eating, sleeping. There is nowhere to go for relief. Even doing nothing takes energy that I don't have.

Secretly I tend to a part of myself that can't be touched. I whisper to it a word of hope a day.
After a while, that part starts to grow.
And then I have the ability to break free inch by inch.
I wish I could describe this process better. Maybe then this comic would be useful. But I think I mostly just get lucky. Many people get caught and never escape.
Some monsters you can make friends with. Some you can't
I think healing begins when we start to run towards something rather than away from the things that bring us fear.

In utopia depression wouldn't be called depression
but extra emotional sensitivity.

In utopia PTSD wouldn't be called PTSD
but time travel.

In utopia borderline personality disorder
wouldn't be called BPD
but instead the power to hold
many different forces at once.

In this world though,
health care industry talks in terms of A Cure,
always talks about medicating us enough
to pass as their definition of normal.

But we don't need a cure and
we don't need to be normal.
We have infinite potential to thrive
just as we are.
In utopia mental illness would still exist
but our talents would be worked with
instead of against.
In utopia, when it was our turn again
to hold the sadness and weight of the world,
our neighbors would show up at our doorstep
with armfuls of food and love
and thank us for doing all that hardwork
and for still surviving.

Thank you for reading my zine! After quite a few years I finally made it to #10. Writing these has allowed me the space to learn and remember what keeps me alive and reflect on many ripples in the big ocean known as "Mental Health." I expect the next 10 will be just as weirdly pasted together but just as fun for me to make. Maybe fun is the wrong word. Anyways, thank you for supporting my work. ♡♡♡ -Shea

Microcosm Publishing is Portland's most diversified publishing house and distributor with a focus on the colorful, authentic, and empowering. Our books and zines have put your power in your hands since 1996, equipping readers to make positive changes in their lives and in the world around them. Microcosm emphasizes skill-building, showing hidden histories, and fostering creativity through challenging conventional publishing wisdom with books and bookettes about DIY skills, food, bicycling, gender, self-care, and social justice. What was once a distro and record label was started by Joe Biel in his bedroom and has become among the oldest independent publishing houses in Portland, OR. We are a politically moderate, centrist publisher in a world that has inched to the right for the past 80 years.